The Treehouse Club

By Wendy Blaxland
Illustrated by Craig Smith

Rigby

CLUB RULES
1. No boys.
2. Come in the window.
3. Use the password.

These are our club rules.

1 No boys.

2 Come in the window.

3 Use the password.

Isabelle's little brother wanted to come in.
"No boys!" we said.

He was sad.
We looked at each other.

"He's a bit little," said Ruth.
"Let's see. Can we change the rule?"

CLUB RULE
1. No boys. if we let them.
me in the
e the pas

We made a new rule:
Boys, if we let them.

7

Sara wanted to come up the ladder.
"Come in the window," we said.

8

She was sad.
We looked at each other.

"She's a bit scared," said Anna.
"Let's see. Can we change the rule?"

We made a new rule:
Come in the window, if you can.

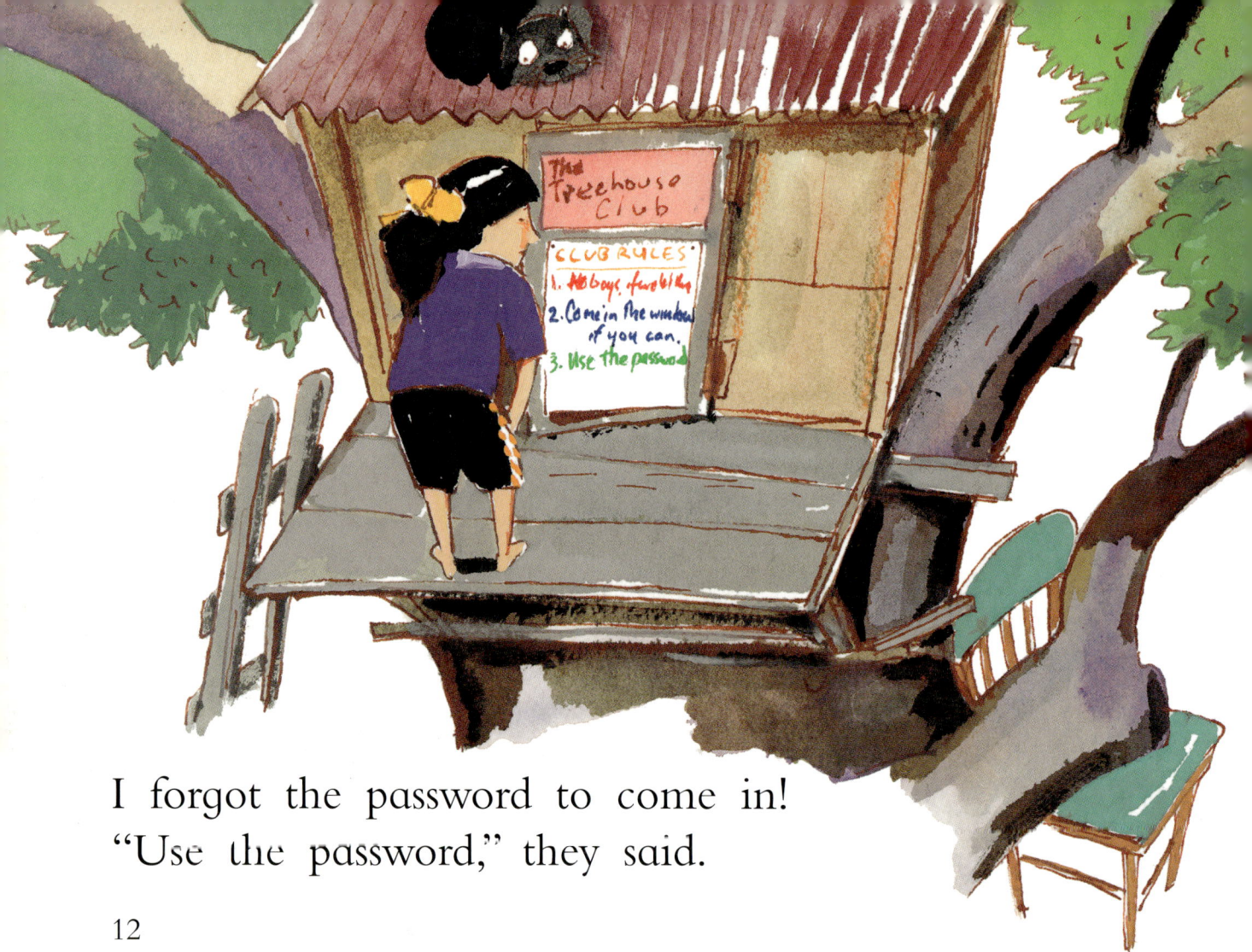

I forgot the password to come in!
"Use the password," they said.

I was sad.
They looked at each other.

"You're a bit forgetful," said Isabelle.
"Let's see. Can we change the rule?"

We made a new rule:
Use the password, if you can.

It's a good club.
We keep all the rules…
when we can!